#BLACKLIVESMATTER

#BlackLivesMatter began in 2013 as a response to the acquittal of Trayvon Martin's murderer. Organizers Alicia Garza, Patrisse Cullors, and Opal Tometi wanted to end violence—particularly police violence—against Black Americans.

Black Lives Matter is a collective of organizations and activists railing against Black oppression and advocating for criminal justice reform. With each new incident of deadly force by police, their fight for justice strengthened, culminating in the George Floyd protests.

On May 25, 2020, Minneapolis police officer Derek Chauvin knelt on the neck of George Floyd, a Black man in his custody, for 8 minutes and 46 seconds, ignoring Floyd's pleas for help, until he was dead. Captured bystander video went viral on social media, and Black Lives Matter activists quickly mobilized to protest the injustice. In cities and towns across the country and around the world, people of all races took to the streets to denounce George Floyd's murder and demand police reform.

For the first time since its inception, Black Lives Matter enjoyed support from a majority of Americans. In the past, the movement had spurred countermovements such as #AllLivesMatter, #BlueLivesMatter, and even #WhiteLivesMatter. Currently, the average number of tweets tagged with the hashtag #BlackLivesMatter averages 3.7 million per day. **

** As of May 2021

#METOO

When it comes to effecting change, #MeToo is without a doubt one of the most successful hashtags ever created. But that didn't happen overnight.

In 2006, activist Tarana Burke used the phrase "me too" on MySpace to encourage and empower survivors of sexual abuse and harassment. Eleven years later, actress Alyssa Milano used the words to support victims of movie producer Harvey Weinstein, whose abhorrent behavior toward young women had long been Hollywood's dirty little secret. The response to Milano's tweet was immense and proved that sexual harassment can and does happen to all kinds of people in all kinds of professions.

Thanks to the high profile of the celebrities who spoke out, #MeToo quickly spread around the world. Weinstein was convicted and imprisoned. Dozens of other high-profile men who had also behaved badly lost their jobs.

But millions of women who don't have the benefit of access to the press and a devoted fanbase continue to suffer fear and discrimination in the workplace. Burke acknowledges the importance of Milano's role in sparking a global movement while cautioning that even though a few men in the spotlight have been held accountable, there is still much work to be done in changing the culture.

#TAKEAKNEE

In 2016, NFL quarterback Colin Kaepernick attracted some attention when he remained seated during the national anthem to protest the mistreatment of Black people in America. "I am not going to stand up to show pride in a flag for a country that oppresses black people and people of color," he explained.

On the advice of former Green Beret and Seattle Seahawk Nate Boyer, Kaepernick began taking a knee next to his teammates as they rose for the national anthem before each game. This gesture is used by soldiers to show respect for a fallen brother-in-arms, but many football fans criticized Kaepernick because they believed he was disrespecting the US flag.

But many rushed to support his bravery. Sales of Kaepernick's team jersey soared. Even non-football fans suddenly knew who he was and what he was fighting for.

Since January 2017, Colin Kaepernick has been a player without a team. But there is no doubt that he was a part of something more important than football. Within a few years, athletes in other sports would stage boycotts and strikes to send a message about systemic racism and police brutality in America.

#EARTHDAY

Earth Day predates the use of hashtags by several decades, but social media has helped the movement grow with the times.

The first Earth Day was held on April 22, 1970. It was the creation of Wisconsin senator Gaylord Nelson, who recruited activist Denis Hayes to organize college campus teach-ins to raise consciousness about the air and water pollution crises in the country. Earth Day's reach extended beyond college students, inspiring a public who shared concerns about the state of the planet after decades of industrialization and corporate unaccountability. In cities across the country, 20 million Americans demonstrated on behalf of the planet. A new environmental movement was born.

That first Earth Day spawned the establishment of the Environmental Protection Agency. The EPA would be responsible for a host of important legislation that protected Americans, wildlife, and the natural world.

Earth Day went global in 1990, gaining more support from governments and citizens around the world. A decade later, issues such as climate change and clean energy would come to the forefront. In 2016, Earth Day was chosen as the date when leaders from 175 nations would sign the revolutionary Paris Agreement.

#RAISETHEMW

Using the hashtag #RaiseTheMW, Raisetheminimumwage.org is a campaign driven by the National Employment Law Project. Wages have remained criminally low in the United States for the past 40 years.

After adjusting for inflation, today's wages have the same purchasing power as wages in 1978! Sadly, wage gains have been enjoyed by only the highest-paid workers.

In those 40 years, the minimum wage has lost 30% of its value and has been stuck at $7.25 (around $15,000/year for a full-time worker) for nearly 15 years, while the cost of living has continued to rise steadily. Many people can no longer get by on one or even two minimum-wage jobs.

In 2012, fast food workers in New York City walked off their jobs and demanded an hourly wage of $15 as well as a union. This action inspired demonstrations around the country and resulted in minimum wage increases on many local and state levels.

But the US government has yet to pass legislation that would mandate a $15 minimum wage on the federal level. In January 2021, the Raise the Wage Act was introduced as part of a COVID-19 relief bill, but it failed to pass in the Senate.

#YESALLWOMEN

The hashtag and subsequent social media campaign #YesAllWomen was a response to 2014's Isla Vista killings, in which a man who had published a manifesto declaring his hatred for women because they had rejected him went on a killing spree.

Specifically, the hashtag was a direct response to another hashtag—#NotAllMen—that had been around for a while but had gone viral after the attacks.

#NotAllMen was initially used to make the point that not all men think or behave in the way the Isla Vista killer did, but it was roundly rejected as a tone-deaf take on the situation. #YesAllWomen was tweeted out to shift the focus back on women and the misogyny, harassment, and violence that is regularly directed at them as a result of a culture of toxic masculinity.

#YesAllWomen became a tool for women to share their experiences with regard to that culture, most of which are seemingly banal and so ingrained in our everyday lives that you might miss them if you weren't looking. Women are constantly told not to dress provocatively, not to anger men, not to trust men—the message being that it's a man's world. The angry reaction to the killings with #NotAllMen proves that all too well.

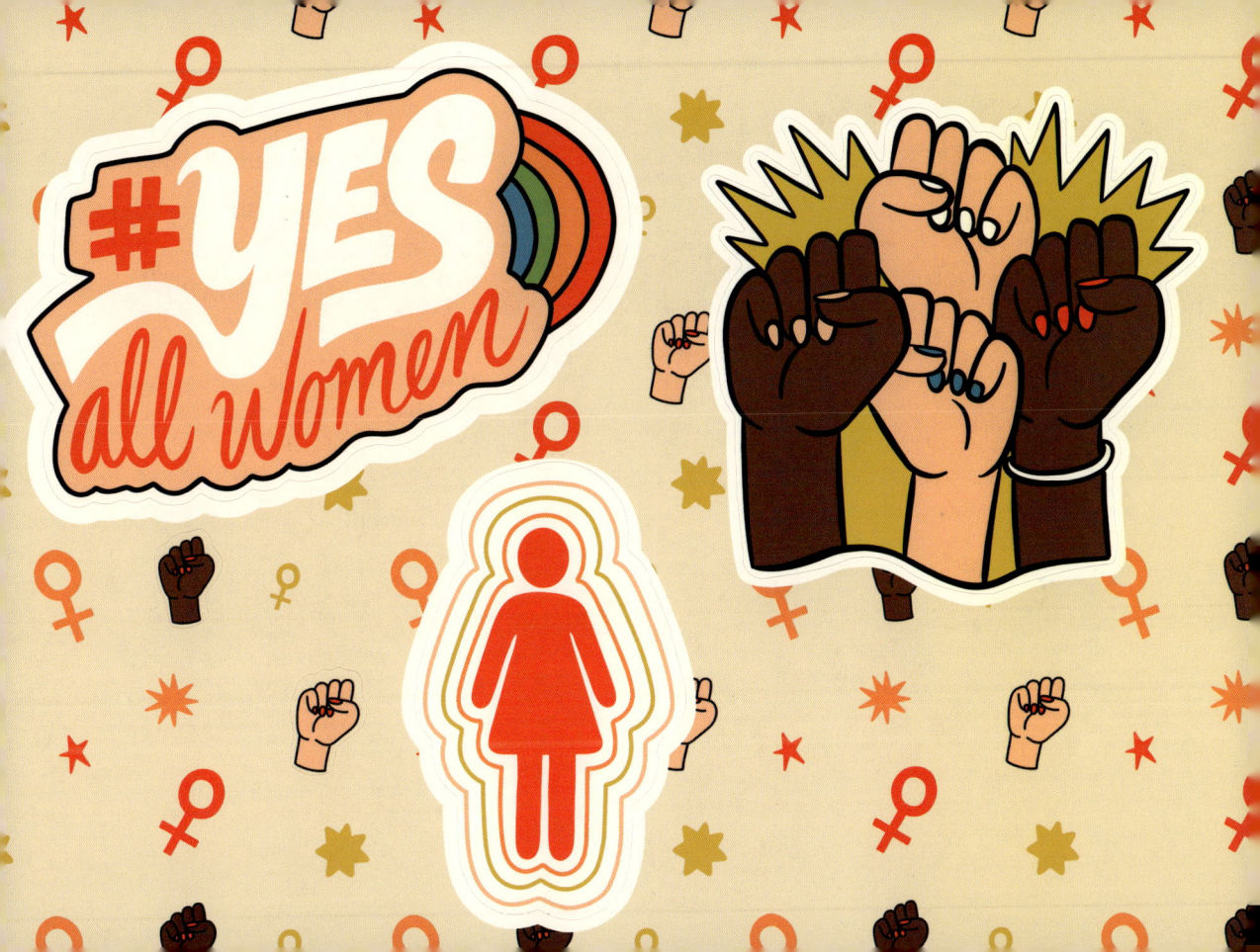

#LOVEWINS

When the Supreme Court of the United States ruled in favor of legalizing same-sex marriage on June 26, 2015, millions of supporters across the country celebrated.

The case was *Obergefell v. Hodges*, and the decision that state bans on same-sex marriage were unconstitutional was by the narrowest margin: 5–4. Despite this, public opinion toward same-sex marriage had shifted steadily in the United States over the previous years. (President Barack Obama announced that the monumental decision "affirms what millions of Americans already believe in their hearts.")

The Human Rights Campaign, a leading LGBTQ+ civil rights organization, used the hashtag #LoveWins to celebrate the landmark Supreme Court decision and flooded social media with posts to rally and inspire users. This campaign was incredibly effective.

Celebrities, as well as President Obama himself, shared the hashtag with their legions of followers. So did many organizations and corporations.

Obergefell v. Hodges was an important Supreme Court decision, but it also tapped into the emotions of the country—and the world. #LoveWins was certainly not the only hashtag to celebrate the ruling, but it was the most widely shared on Instagram and Twitter. Years later, "Love Wins" is still used as shorthand to convey the importance and beauty of the convergence of two fundamental rights: equality and love.

#SAYHERNAME

Malcolm X said it: "The most disrespected person in America is the Black woman."

You've undoubtedly heard the names George Floyd, Freddie Gray, and Eric Garner. The murders of these Black men at the hands of police were widely publicized and protested. But Black women are regularly victims of police mistreatment as well. Often, the brutality toward and murder of Black women is underreported or outright ignored.

That is why the African American Policy Forum created the campaign Say Her Name in 2014. Since then, photos of Black women killed by the police or as a result of police mistreatment have cropped up on social media with the hashtag #SayHerName, a plea to remember the victims and hold police accountable.

Perhaps the best known victim is Breonna Taylor, a Kentucky woman whose fatal shooting by the police was a result of a raid on her apartment that went horribly wrong. None of the officers involved in the shooting were indicted, despite calls for #JusticeForBreonnaTaylor, although Taylor's family was awarded $12 million in a wrongful death lawsuit.

#FIREDRILLFRIDAYS

#FireDrillFridays is the brainchild of actress and activist Jane Fonda and Greenpeace director Annie Leonard.

Desperately concerned about the state of the environment and about the unwillingness of our leaders to do something about it, Fonda sought a way to effect change. Inspired by Greta Thunberg's School Strike for Climate Fridays, Fire Drill Fridays was a weekly protest in Washington, DC, that concerned different aspects of the climate crisis, each event ending in a civil disobedience arrest by police.

Fonda's celebrity attracted other big names to join her in the protests. They stood side by side with a variety of concerned American activists, all willing to go to jail for their beliefs.

The group made pointed demands, such as the adoption by Congress of the Green New Deal and implementation of a plan to shift to clean energy sources.

Fire Drill Fridays expanded to protests in other portions of the United States. Even the pandemic didn't slow down the mission of the group. Fonda maintained a steady presence on social media and made public appearances, holding leaders accountable and convincing anyone who would listen that the planet is in a climate emergency.

#CLIMATECHANGEISREAL

It seems impossible to believe, but there are still many climate change deniers in the world. Even with the increasing frequency of disastrous extreme weather events, rising global temperatures, and discouraging projections from scientists, some people refuse to believe that climate change exists.

It is unclear whether this denial comes from an inability to understand scientific facts or from an ability to ignore them in the interest of making money from things that contribute to the destruction of our planet.

The #ClimateChangeIsReal campaign launched in 2015. It was tweeted and retweeted by government leaders, global corporations, celebrities, and citizens from both sides of the aisle, reaching an estimated 265 million people. But even with the momentum of the hashtag, deniers continued to deny, and soon enough a new administration was in the White House, pulling out of the Paris Climate Agreement and doubling down on a commitment to fossil fuels. Climate change deniers felt free to broadcast their message loudly once again.

Extreme weather events have continued, and even with a new president elected in 2020 who is committed to the environment, it could be too late to undo the damage. Still, the message rings true: #ClimateChangeIsReal. Just open your eyes and look around.

#TIMESUP

In 2018, after the horrifying extent of movie producer Harvey Weinstein's criminal behavior was uncovered, a group of women in the entertainment business decided that enough was enough.

Building on the momentum of the #MeToo movement, which amplified the rampant problem of sexual violence against women, #TimesUp sought to take active steps to ensure women's safety and equity in the workplace.

While it was Hollywood actresses and creators in the entertainment industry who got the ball rolling, eventually the movement spread across many professions. In its first year, TIME'S UP raised a whopping $22 million and established a TIME'S UP Legal Defense Fund.

The group advocates for policy changes and for gender parity legislation that would ensure women equal pay and equal opportunities.

TIME'S UP believes that sexual violence against women will continue until steps are taken to eradicate workplace discrimination and to achieve gender equity. The United States has failed to ratify an Equal Rights Amendment for a century. Is now the time?

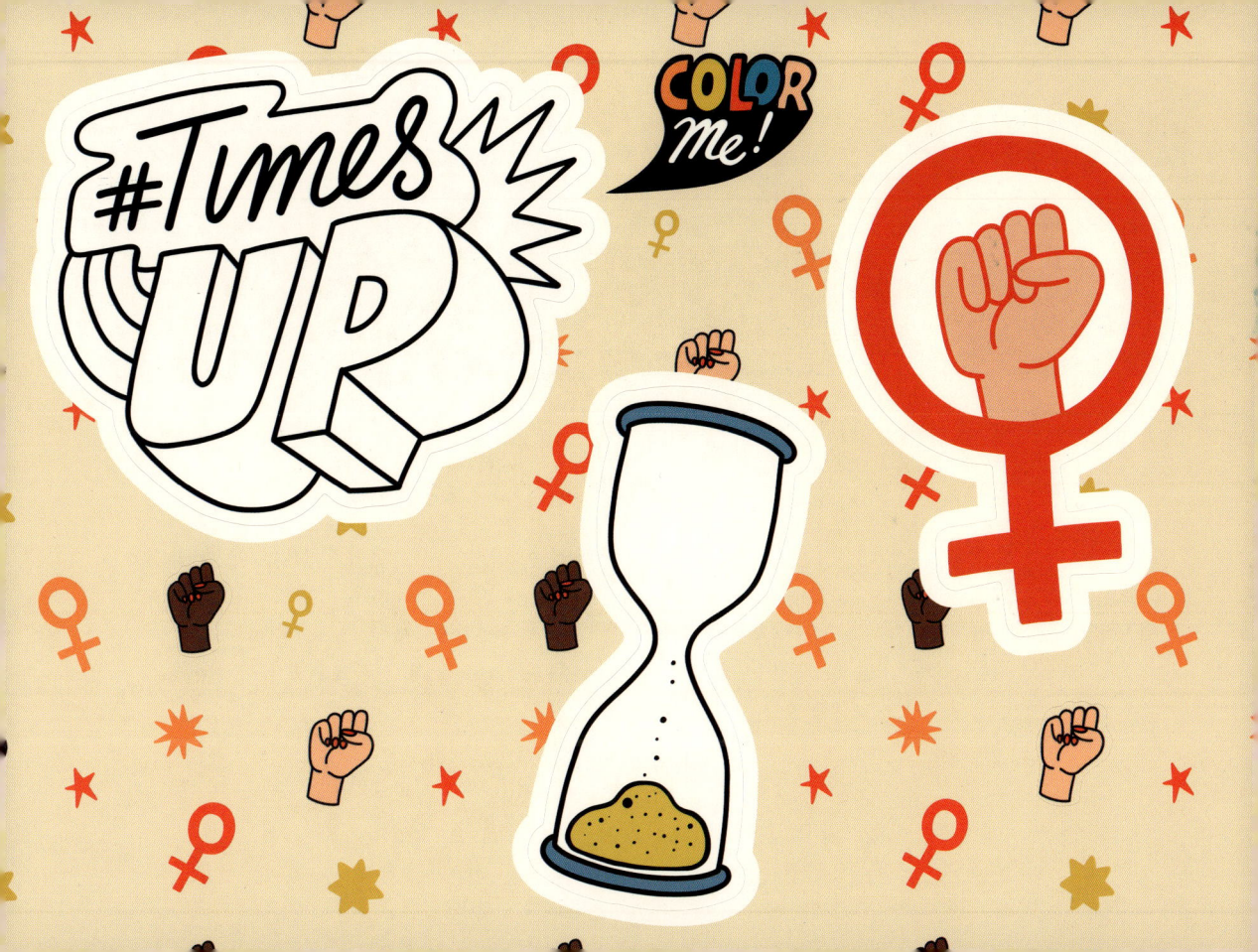

#*GIRLSLIKEUS*

Trans activist Janet Mock created the hashtag #GirlsLikeUs in 2012 as a response to the injustice experienced by CeCe McDonald. McDonald, a trans woman convicted of murder for defending herself in a transphobic attack, was held in a men's prison and initially denied the hormones she required.

Sadly, McDonald's story was not unique. Trans women have historically been subject to harassment, discrimination, and violence, with few consequences.

#GirlsLikeUs quickly became an outlet for trans women to contribute their stories and share information. This expanded into an entire social media network, including Twitter and YouTube, which allowed trans individuals to spread their message beyond their own community.

It also helped to raise the visibility of trans women in society. Outspoken activists like Mock and Laverne Cox have worked tirelessly to fight for trans representation and inclusion. Cox's groundbreaking portrayal of a trans inmate on the television series *Orange Is the New Black* introduced many Americans to the struggles and humanity of trans individuals.

The success of #GirlsLikeUs spawned similar social media movements for other groups, including #BoysLikeUs, where trans men seek support and discuss issues specific to them, and #FolksLikeUs, for nonbinary and gender-nonconforming individuals.

#REFUGEES*WELCOME*

In 2015, Europe experienced an immigration crisis. In that year, approximately one million refugees arrived on European shores.

The majority had fled dangerous circumstances in countries like Syria, Iraq, and Afghanistan and were seeking safe spaces in which to live their lives and raise their families.

The influx sparked a crisis in predominantly stable and peaceful European nations. Germany, Austria, Hungary, and Sweden bore the brunt of asylum seekers, but throngs of migrants traveled across the Mediterranean Sea to Italy and Greece. Thousands died during the journey. Those who made it lived in limbo in makeshift refugee camps. German chancellor Angela Merkel's policy to welcome refugees did not sit well with other EU leaders, who worried that without solving the problem at its root even more migrants would follow and drain the resources of EU member nations. Some countries closed their borders.

Still, NGOs and other organizations willing to help cropped up, finding accommodations for migrants and providing assistance for assimilation. In stark contrast to strict immigration policies issued by several world leaders, the #RefugeesWelcome hashtag went viral. A banner bearing the message was even draped across the base of the Statue of Liberty.

#STOPASIANHATE #STOPAAPIHATE

In late 2019, as COVID-19 began its spread and people around the world were becoming ill and dying, another sickness emerged in the United States: racist acts against Asian Americans.

In truth, discrimination and mistreatment of Asians in America is nearly as old as the United States itself. There was literally a piece of legislation called the Chinese Exclusion Act, after all. But this was 2020. To blame ordinary citizens for a global pandemic simply because of the way they look was both ludicrous and frightening. And violence against Asian Americans had been trending upward in the years leading up to the pandemic.

The hashtags #StopAsianHate and #StopAAPIHate (AAPI is short for Asian/Asian Pacific Islander) aimed to address white supremacism in America and its focus on Asian Americans as a target. Both hashtags are attached to organizations that advocate for education, reporting of attacks, and building a stronger community to stop hate in its tracks.

#PRIDE

Unlike #LoveWins and #LoveIsLove, which reference specific events, #Pride is a general hashtag that celebrates LGBTQ+ experiences on social media, particularly during Pride Month in June, which honors those who participated in the Stonewall Riots.

The Stonewall Inn was a gay bar located in New York City's Greenwich Village. At a time when open homosexuality was not acceptable—or even legal—gay bars provided a somewhat safe space. In New York, most were owned by the Mafia, which meant that every now and then police conducted a routine raid on the bars. During one such raid on June 28, 1969, bar patrons fought back and police lost control of the situation. Tensions crackled throughout the neighborhood, and protests and scuffles broke out for the next six days.

The Stonewall Riots sparked several important gay rights organizations and invigorated LGBTQ+ activism. The event is largely seen as the genesis of the modern gay rights movement, one that allowed millions of people around the world to show their #Pride.

Today, the Stonewall Inn is a registered historic landmark and is still in operation.

#LOVEISLOVE

The hashtag #LoveIsLove, which began trending in 2016, uses the universal experience of love to promote a message of LGBTQ+ acceptance. After all, how could anyone who cares about love devalue or discriminate against someone who simply wants to love whom they love?

The message seems designed to counter haters with love, an emotion they can relate to. Rather than getting into a broader argument about queer rights, it highlights the humanity of LGBTQ+ individuals.

And who could argue with a sentiment as beautiful as #LoveIsLove? It turns out, perhaps surprisingly, that some LGBTQ+ advocates feel the slogan is patronizing and that people should accept the queer community for all that they are, without the qualifier of love.

In his 2016 Tony Award acceptance speech, *Hamilton* creator Lin-Manuel Miranda memorably paid tribute to the victims of a mass shooting at a gay nightclub in Orlando, saying, "Love is love is love is love is love is love is love, cannot be killed or swept aside."

#WENEEDDIVERSEBOOKS

Think back to the childhood books that you loved most. Did you relate to the characters, or did you wish someone would write a story about a kid just like you?

There is a critical lack of diversity in book publishing, particularly children's book publishing. Astonishingly, the main characters of children's books are more likely to be animals than they are humans from diverse backgrounds! This is the issue at the heart of the hashtag #WeNeedDiverseBooks.

When children see themselves represented in a book, they connect with the story and feel their value in the world. When they see characters who are not like them, say someone of another race or gender or who is differently abled, they learn understanding and compassion for a variety of cultural experiences.

But it's about more than book characters. The publishing industry, too, has a diversity problem. First tweeted out by authors Ellen Oh and Malinda Lo in 2014, #WeNeedDiverseBooks is an example of a simple hashtag that generated inspiration to spawn an organization that is working hard to effect change. The hashtag alone isn't enough, though. Oh recognizes that there is a long way to go and looks forward to a day when her campaign is not needed.

#TAKEONHATE

Bias and discrimination, including hate crimes, against Arab and Muslim Americans were triggered after 9/11 and have not waned in subsequent decades.

The National Network for Arab American Communities (NNAAC) launched the organization Take on Hate in 2014 to address the issue, making use of the hashtag #TakeOnHate on various social media platforms to boost messages of positivity about Arab Americans and Muslim Americans.

Take on Hate advocates for policy changes on the federal level and at the local level. It prioritizes education and awareness of the important contributions this community makes to our society. Media depictions of Arab and Muslim Americans do much to degrade the public's perception of the community. Take on Hate rallies against media bias and calls out negative portrayals, asking the media to simply do better.

The campaign also stands against hatred toward all communities. It asks Arab Americans and Muslim Americans, as well as all Americans opposed to bigotry, to take a stand and actively take on hate.

#STOPTHESTIGMA

Although nearly one in five Americans lives with a mental illness, according to the National Institute of Mental Health, stigma and discrimination are still widespread enough that many people who need help are too ashamed or afraid to seek it. Many organizations that advocate for mental health awareness have launched campaigns featuring the hashtag #StopTheStigma.

The principle behind #StopTheStigma is that eliminating shame associated with mental health will also eliminate forces that work to obstruct people from obtaining information, diagnoses, and treatment. Education campaigns convey warning signs, steps to take, and perhaps most important, the fact that mental illness is relatively common.

#StopTheStigma was frequently used during the COVID-19 pandemic and quarantine, when people living with mental illness were especially vulnerable and people who may not have been aware of mental health issues were suddenly faced with enormous challenges such as illness, death, loneliness, and isolation. Perhaps the universality of the situation encouraged more people to end the stigma associated with mental illness.

#TRANSISBEAUTIFUL

#TransIsBeautiful is a hashtag created in 2015 by transgender actress and activist Laverne Cox.

Famous for her revolutionary portrayal of a trans inmate in the Netflix series *Orange Is the New Black*, Cox was inspired to start the hashtag when she posed nude for a photo shoot. That experience left her with a determination to be authentic, and she challenged all trans people to find that authenticity as well. Years after she started the hashtag, Cox continues to end most of her social media posts with the message #TransIsBeautiful.

At the 2015 Fashion Media Awards, Cox explained the inspiration behind the hashtag: "I would like to encourage every single one of you in this room to join with me in showing the world that trans is beautiful in terms of how we cover trans stories and diverse stories in general. There are so many different kinds of beauty in the world that I want to celebrate, and I know you want to celebrate it, too."

#CELEBRATEMYSIZE

> **#CelebrateMySize is just one of several hashtags that promote body positivity.** These networks have made great strides in generating awareness and acceptance of different body types, going a long way toward promoting social change.

Plus Model Magazine created the #CelebrateMySize hashtag as a celebration of curvy bodies. The magazine shared images of curvy women on its Instagram account and published reader accounts of why they love their curves.

Our media culture is constantly sending the message that women need to look a certain way—namely small and thin. Magazine tutorials on how to get a summer body or what to do to fit into that pair of jeans are out of touch and damaging. If you have a body and it's summer, then you have a summer body! If you want to fit into a certain style of jeans, just find the proper size and wear them!

By changing the narrative and imploring women to rethink beauty standards, #CelebrateMySize encourages the most important thing of all: acceptance of all that our bodies do for us, which is what makes them beautiful in the first place.

#NEVERAGAIN

On February 14, 2018, a former student entered Marjory Stoneman Douglas High School in Parkland, Florida, and went on a shooting rampage. When all was said and done, 17 students and staff were dead.

The tragedy sparked an immediate call to action, with students imploring lawmakers to take a stand against gun violence. A group of impassioned and media-savvy MSD students gave interviews to top news outlets, pleading for stricter gun control legislation. One student, Cameron Kasky, launched the hashtag #NeverAgain.

Fueled by momentum, these student activists planned the March for Our Lives rally in the nation's capitol. They met with President Trump and shared their tales of terror with him, hoping to change his position. They pressured politicians in Florida and boycotted individuals and businesses who supported the National Rifle Association (NRA).

March for Our Lives was held in Washington, DC, and cities across the country and around the world. An estimated one to two million people participated in the event, including some very big celebrity names who supported the cause.

On the one-month anniversary of the Parkland shootings, thousands of students across the country took part in a scheduled school walkout, demanding action against gun violence and vowing #NeverAgain.

#NOTONEMORE

#NotOneMore is a plea aimed directly at lawmakers. The three words were chanted out of frustration and grief by Richard Martinez, whose son was murdered in a 2014 attack known as the Isla Vista Killings.

Aware that his words had resonated with the public, Martinez urged citizens to take a stand. He told the press, "Today, I'm going to ask every person I can find to send a postcard to every politician with three words on it: 'Not one more.'"

It isn't easy for one man to make a difference, but sometimes all that is needed is to plant the seed. Everytown for Gun Safety, an influential nonprofit organization financed by former New York City mayor Michael Bloomberg, took notice of Martinez's plea and used its power to publicize the campaign in the press and over social media. In the next few weeks, more than 100,000 tweets used the hashtag #NotOneMore. Supporters, including celebrities such as Julianne Moore and Snoop Dogg, posted photos of themselves holding signs bearing the hashtag.

#HEFORSHE

In the unending quest for gender equality, there's no doubt that women have done the heavy lifting. But women can't do it alone, nor should they have to.

In order to create a world in which women enjoy the same wages, status, and safety of their male counterparts, men must also be on board. After all, gender inequality is a human rights issue. It affects everyone.

#HeForShe is the hashtag used in a United Nations global campaign bearing the same name that promotes gender equality and solidarity. It encourages boys and men to actively reject stereotypes that have a negative effect on women and to help women succeed in the professional, economic, family, and community realms.

The World Economic Forum predicts that none of us will see gender parity in our lifetime. Their Global Gender Gap Report predicts that it will take nearly 100 years to close the gender gap. HeForShe understands that achieving gender parity won't happen overnight. It is committed to a long haul, first asking for commitment, then providing resources for redefining gender roles and concrete steps to take in order to make this world more equitable for all.

#THISISWHATDISABILITYLOOKSLIKE

#ThisIsWhatDisabilityLooksLike is a movement designed to flood social media with authentic and largely positive representations of people living with disabilities.

According to the Centers for Disease Control, 1 in 4 Americans lives with some type of disability that impacts major life activities. (Lack of mobility is the most common disability.) Yet until disability affects them directly, most Americans do all that they can to ignore it. And that occurs on an institutional level as well. Despite the passage of the Americans with Disability Act (1990), accessibility is still an impediment for many people.

It's no wonder, then, that many people who live with disabilities feel invisible. While disability activists and movements like #ThisIsWhatDisabilityLooksLike have gone a long way toward bringing awareness to disability rights, people of color argue that they are not included in much of this work.

Another hashtag, #SayTheWord, addresses the possibly well-intentioned but insensitive inclination to reject the word "disabled" in favor of "differently abled." Many in the disabled community believe that substitution attempts to erase disability and allows the speaker to deny acknowledgement of the challenges faced by people who live with disabilities as well as the accomplishments they make.

#STOPFUNDINGHATE

Stop Funding Hate was launched by Richard Wilson in 2016 in the UK as a tool to promote ethical advertising. Wilson was struck by a barrage of anti-immigrant news stories in the British press and connected this narrative to increasing violence and hate crimes on the streets.

These stories capitalizing on fear and hatred were obviously selling newspapers, particularly the notorious British tabloids, or else the papers would not have run them so incessantly. Wilson believed that hitting them where it hurts—that is, their advertising dollars—might make them reconsider their irresponsible editorial strategy. He called on readers to take to social media and, using #StopFundingHate, put pressure on the companies that advertise in these papers to take a stand against hate and pull out.

#StopFundingHate is truly a campaign for the people, empowering individuals to make a difference on a direct level without waiting for government involvement. Critics argue that this is a form of censorship, where advertisers and, indirectly, readers can affect a news organization's editorial content. #StopFundingHate believes that its model of making hate unprofitable is working: In just three years, the number of anti-immigrant stories on the front page of UK newspapers dropped from 100 to 0.

#WOMENSMARCH

January 21, 2017, was the first full day of Donald J. Trump's presidency. After an underwhelming inauguration celebration turnout the day earlier, on this day Washington, DC, was flooded with millions of women and their allies.

They were protesting misogyny, inequality, and toxic masculinity. And they were protesting the president of the United States.

Trump had been elected in spite of controversial rhetoric on many subjects, including mistreatment and disrespect of women. The most damning was a hot mic moment from an *Access Hollywood* segment in which Trump was caught bragging about sexual harassment. The clip was pulled out of the vault and rebroadcast for all to hear.

Trump's election was the final straw for millions of women who were tired of living in a culture that excused away behavior like Trump's. It was enough to mobilize millions of women (and men) to take to the streets to demonstrate against the president and all that he stood for. #WomensMarch and #WhyIMarch became trending hashtags, and the march became a catalyst for a resistance movement.

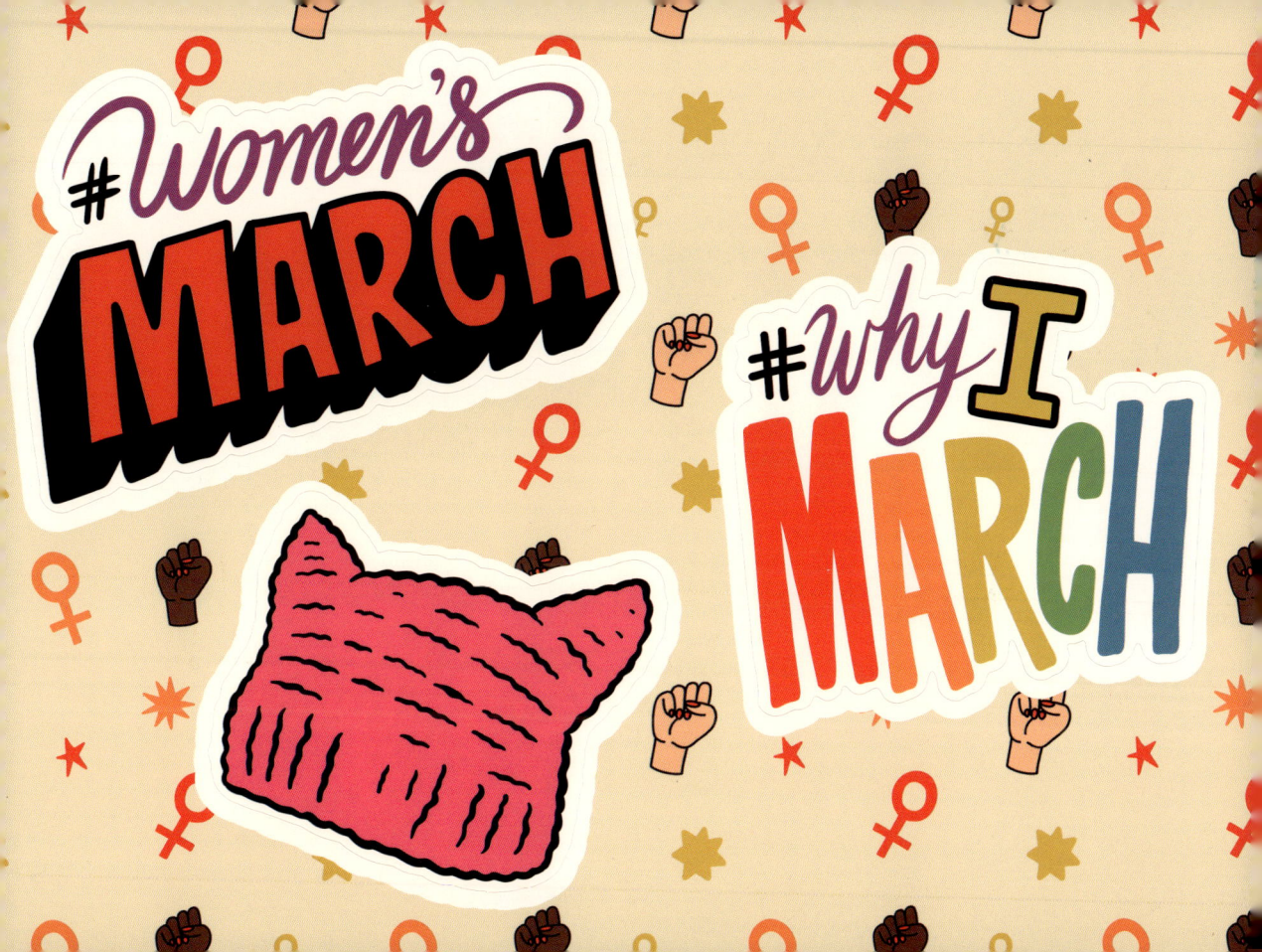

#BLACKGIRLMAGIC/#BLACKBOYJOY

"Black girl magic" seems like a phrase that's been in use forever, but in fact it was created in 2013 by teacher, writer, and social media influencer CaShawn Thompson, who used the hashtag #BlackGirlMagic to celebrate Black excellence, uplift Black women, and amplify their accomplishments. The term became ubiquitous, used in popular culture and academia alike.

#BlackGirlMagic has its critics, of course. Some feel that it presents the misconception that Black women are superhuman and minimizes the very real challenges they must overcome to achieve excellence.

Although it's not connected to a specific movement, #BlackBoyJoy is a popular hashtag that simply highlights moments of lightness and joy in Black boys' (and Black men's) lives. The reason #BlackBoyJoy is important is that, amid all of the things that Black boys and men are taught about navigating through a society that is decidedly stacked against them, they should be allowed to experience beautiful moments of innocence and pure joy like anyone else.

#UNDOCUMENTEDANDUNAFRAID

An estimated one to two million minors in America are undocumented, neither US citizens nor of legal immigrant status. They have been brought into the US by parents or other family who have immigrated illegally, raised as Americans but without the guarantee of a future as Americans.

Undocumented children often are embarrassed by their situations and live in fear of the bottom dropping out of their lives. Maybe their parents will be deported and they will be alone. Maybe when they reach adulthood they will be sent back to a country they've never really known. This can lead to severe anxiety, depression, and even suicide.

Many have lived in the shadows, afraid to call attention to themselves in a country that may turn its back on them. But that all began to change as legislation was passed that provided undocumented minors—called Dreamers—with the promise of certain rights and protections.

#UndocumentedAndUnafraid is a social media hashtag that became a tool for Dreamers to come out, connect with others, and embrace the unique situations they face. Not only does it bring awareness to their challenges and the need for better policies, but it also is a form of empowerment for these Americans.

#MUSLIMSARENOTTERRORIST

#MuslimsAreNotTerrorist first began trending in November 2015 after a series of terror attacks in Paris left 130 dead and hundreds wounded.

The shootings and bombings were carried out by members of ISIS in several locations throughout the city, including a stadium holding a soccer game, a sold-out concert hall, and several restaurants. Sadly, they were not the first terror attacks to be experienced in Paris that year.

Soon after the day of terror, Muslims around the world as well as their allies began tweeting #MuslimsAreNotTerrorist and using the hashtag on other social media platforms to counter Islamophobia and anti-Muslim sentiments that arose as a result of the attacks. One such message read, "I am a Muslim/Islam is perfect, but i am not/If i make mistake, blame me, but not Religion."

The hashtag continues to be used in an attempt to normalize Islam to those to whom it might seem foreign and to present positive representation of Muslims as loving, hardworking, respectable citizens around the world.

#NOTINMYNAME

#NotInMyName is a hashtag that has been used to convey several different messages.

In 2014, London's Active Change Foundation began the #NotInMyName campaign as a way to protest ISIS's actions and misrepresentation of the Islamic religion. The campaign encouraged British Muslims to take to social media to reject ISIS's violence in the name of Islam and to denounce their ideology of hate.

In 2018, South African activists Siyabulela Jentile and Themba Masango formed the civil rights movement #NotInMyName to fight rampant gender-based violence in that country. South Africa's femicide rate is about five times higher than the global average, and there are an average more than 100 reported rapes every day. #NotInMyName calls on men to take responsibility for these shocking statistics and to put an end to the abuse they inflict on women.

In 2021, a group of women living in Jerusalem used the hashtag to promote love and patience amid violent clashes between Jews and Arabs who live in mixed towns.

#MARCHFOROURLIVES

One month after the shooting at Marjory Stoneman Douglas High School in Parkland, Florida, students organized and led the March for Our Lives, a demonstration against gun violence.

The event took place in Washington, DC, and in other locations across the country, and it was one of the largest—if not the largest—youth protests since the Vietnam era.

#MarchForOurLives continues to fight for policies to prevent gun violence, including registering new voters all over the country. The organization has demanded that the US government agree to its Peace Plan for a Safer America by taking six bold steps it calls C.H.A.N.G.E. in order to address this national epidemic.

These are:
1. **C**hange the standards of gun ownership
2. **H**alve the rate of gun deaths in 10 years
3. **A**ccountability for the gun lobby and industry
4. **N**ame a director of gun violence prevention
5. **G**enerate community-based solutions
6. **E**mpower the next generation

The group has pledged to pressure America's leaders, whose efforts to stop rampant gun violence in America have been inadequate at best and nonexistent at worst, in an effort to stop tragedies like the one at Marjory Stoneman Douglas.

#STOPSEPARATINGFAMILIES

One of the Trump administration's first priorities after the president was inaugurated in 2017 was cracking down on immigration. The most famous was his campaign pledge to "build a wall" to keep migrants from crossing the US–Mexico border.

But another was strict enforcement of the administration's zero-tolerance policy and the ending of the previous practice of "catch and release" in which a detainee would be released to their family and community to await hearings rather than held in detention.

The result was the separation of countless families. Thousands of children, many of them very young, were placed in custody of the Department of Homeland Security while their parents were jailed. This separation caused terror, anxiety, and quite possibly long-term trauma for the children. The government's policies struck many Americans as antithetical to the tenets the United States was founded on. They protested the Trump administration unrelentingly, and the hashtag #StopSeparatingFamilies trended on social media.

In 2018, the administration gave in to pressure and reversed its zero-tolerance policy. The policy had been unsuccessful, not to mention a huge financial drain on taxpayers. A court ordered the children be returned to their parents.

#STANDWITHSURVIVORS

Someone is sexually assaulted every 68 seconds in the United States, according to the Rape, Abuse, and Incest National Network (RAINN). And only 25 rapists out of every thousand will be imprisoned.

It's no wonder, then, that even though sexual assault is widespread many people who experience it never report it or talk about it at all. That can be the result of fear, shame, or lack of trust in the system. But pushing down that trauma has countless long-term negative effects, including anxiety, depression, isolation, and declining performance at school and work.

Acknowledging and sharing survivor stories helps other victims come to terms with the traumas they've experienced. The hashtag #StandWithSurvivors is a way of showing support for survivors of sexual assault. Social media can be a valuable way to connect survivors with help as well as a way to educate your social network about the issue.

Sexual assault is a problem that affects everyone in one way or another. It is important to stand in solidarity with survivors. #StandWithSurvivors.

#GETOUTTHEVOTE

Did you know that voting can become a habit? Research shows that voting in one election sets a precedent for voting in subsequent elections.

But sadly many Americans never get around to that first vote. #GetOutTheVote, or #GOTV, is an umbrella term employed for voting campaigns by organizations such as Rock the Vote and Vote.org.

These organizations are interested in registering voters and encouraging them to vote in local and federal elections. They develop strategies that address any specific obstacles that might impede voting in order to draw as many voters as possible. In theory, these campaigns are nonpartisan, although they do often reveal an agenda by targeting certain demographics or areas. Get Out the Vote campaigns have been conducted worldwide, as well.

One of the most fundamental rights and responsibilities Americans enjoy is the right to cast a vote to elect government representation. Why so many people squander that privilege is anybody's guess. But #GetOutTheVote campaigns are working hard to ensure that increasingly more people understand its importance.

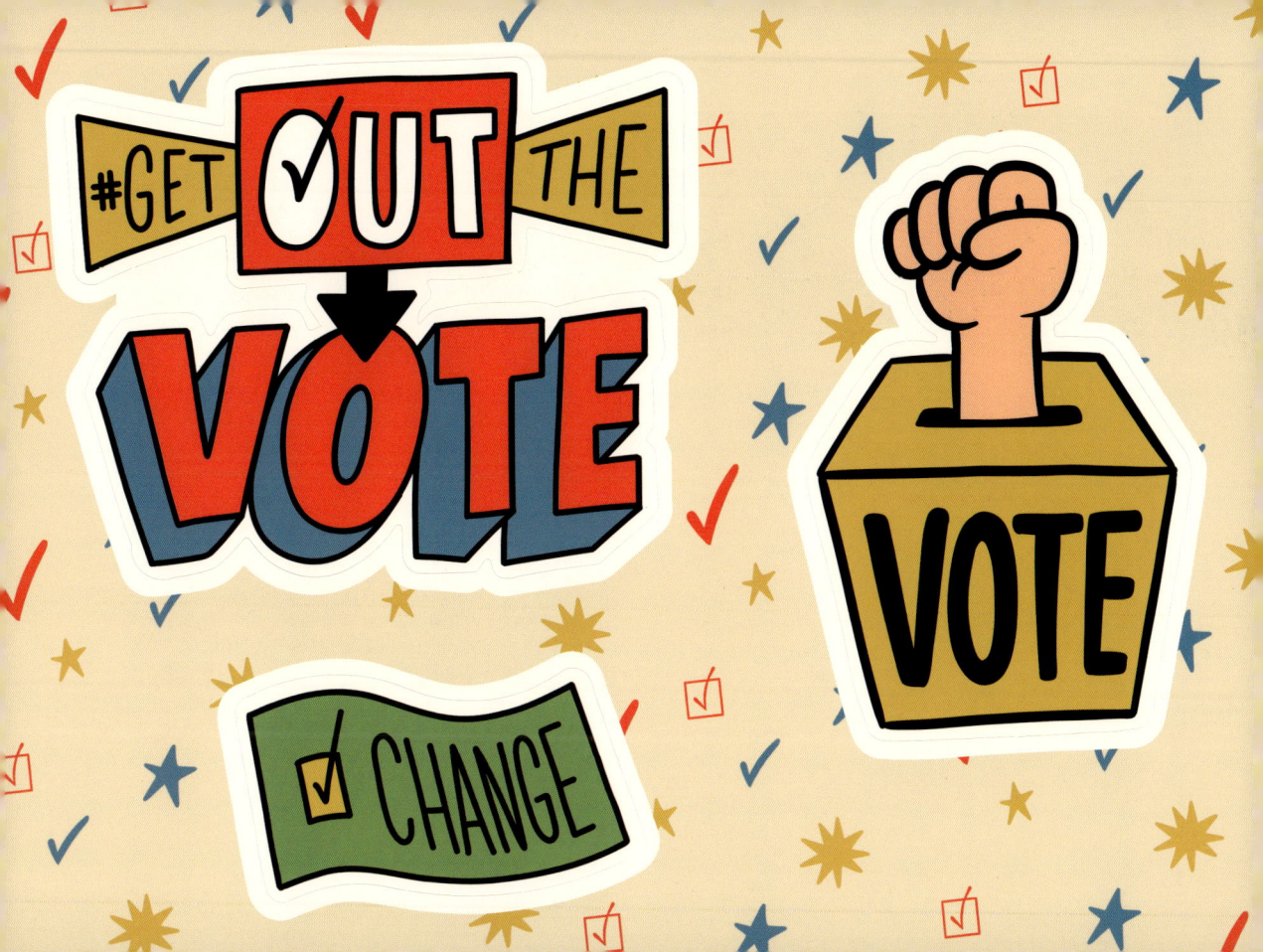

#WORLDWATERDAY

Chances are, you rarely think about water. When you turn on the tap, it is there for you. When you're out and feeling parched, you can easily buy a bottle of it to quench your thirst.

If your lawn is brown, you can turn on the sprinklers to revive it. We waste an awful lot of water without considering what a precious commodity it actually is.

There are plenty of people in the world who don't have enough of it, or what they do have is undrinkable. In fact, a whopping 2.2 billion people in our world don't have access to safe water. And thanks to climate change, those of us who have it now might have a lot less of it in the future.

Recognizing access to clean water as a basic human right, the United Nations General Assembly has set a goal to ensure availability and sustainable management of water and sanitation for all by the year 2030. Every year on March 22, the UN promotes #WorldWaterDay, which brings awareness to the planet's water crisis and educates the public on the missions and achievements of various partners working toward meeting their goal.

#ACTTOCHANGE

Once brushed off as a rite of passage, the issue of bullying has been given the attention it deserves in recent years.

Among many anti-bullying campaigns is Act To Change, a public awareness initiative launched by the Obama administration that is dedicated to preventing bullying of Asian American, immigrant, and LGBTQ+ youth. AAPI youth, in particular, may be reticent to report bullying and to ask for help due to cultural or language barriers.

Act To Change stepped up its efforts during the Trump administration, when some bigoted and xenophobic Americans felt empowered to bully, mistreat, and discriminate against ethnic groups. During the COVID-19 pandemic, many blamed the virus on China and took it out on anyone who looked Asian. Act To Change works to empower young people to embrace their unique backgrounds and to celebrate diversity in America.

Social media has allowed bullying to intensify, but it also has opened the door to accessibility and connectivity. For anyone who is being bullied because of the way they look or talk or where they come from, #ActToChange can provide helpful resources.

#BETHECHANGE

#BeTheChange believes that ordinary citizens have the power to make our world a better place. Politicians, tech giants, and corporate CEOs may let us down, but the power of the people is always there.

Through a network of ambassadors and motivational speakers, the organization wants to inspire positivity and possibility, encouraging people to take responsibility for the change they want and need. Be the Change offers workshops and events around the country to teach individuals how to empower themselves to create change.

Be the Change was founded by motivational speaker Anthony Russo after the 2016 shooting of five Dallas police officers. The organization has grown since then (and it's shifted to a more conservative angle, though it still hopes to draw people of all political persuasions), but it has retained its central message. It believes positive change can be achieved with a focus on relationship building, listening, empathy, and personal connections. All of us can #BeTheChange we want to see in the world.

#ENDMASSINCARCERATION

Although crime rates have dropped considerably over the past decades, the United States has nearly 25 percent of the world's prisoners. That is incredible, considering that the US makes up only 5 percent of the global population.

This disproportionate number is the result of decades-long mass incarceration policies that send more people to prison for longer sentences and make sure they keep coming back. It's also thanks to a system that relies on private prisons that are making some individuals very rich.

There are countless negative effects of mass incarceration. Its targets are people of color—particularly young Black men—and as such it affects Black and low-income communities the most. The cycle created by mass incarceration cripples these communities, inhibiting their development and taking away the chance to succeed. Not all crimes deserve prison sentences, and many people believe that there should be a greater emphasis on alternative punishments, like rehabilitation.

#EndMassIncarceration is a way for social media users to bring awareness to the injustice of the legislation and policies that keep America's prisons at full capacity.

#*VOTINGSAVESLIVES*

More than 50 years after the Voting Rights Act of 1965 outlawed discriminatory voting practices aimed at Black Americans, voter suppression is alive and well in the United States.

It especially affects Black and Latino voters. Another thing that affects Black and Latino voters disproportionately is gun violence, though it's certainly not unique to those communities. And yet they find themselves unable to cast a vote—or face enormous challenges in exercising their right to vote—that could make a change to their lives.

The gun violence prevention organizations March for Our Lives, Brady, and Enough Is Enough have joined to advocate for change at the root level, the foundation of democracy, the vote. They believe that working to create a society based on equity and equality is a key step to achieving the ultimate goal of strengthening America's gun laws and ending gun violence to create a safer and more just society for all Americans. The campaign aptly uses the hashtag #VotingSavesLives because a vote literally has the potential to save lives.

#BLACKOWNEDBUSINESS

Even during the dark days of slavery, Black-owned businesses existed and thrived in the United States.

In the 20th century, an increase in Black-owned business establishments was one of the few positive by-products of the Jim Crow laws that enforced racial segregation. Nowadays, corporations and advertisers finally understand the power of the Black customer, and there are more Black entrepreneurs than ever before.

At a time when consumers care deeply about the politics and backgrounds of the companies they buy products from, they have the choice to take a stand, and many consumers are choosing to buy from Black-owned businesses. But these businesses are vulnerable, as evidenced by the onslaught of the COVID-19 pandemic, which forced 40% of Black-owned businesses (compared to 17% of white-owned businesses) to close in 2020. That year, people also railed against systemic racism and the mistreatment of Black people in the United States. They showed support by marching and protesting, but they also promoted Black-owned businesses by using the hashtag #BlackOwnedBusiness.

The effort produced a spike in sales for these stores, services, and restaurants, albeit a short-lived one. Whether it's with your dollars or your social media accounts, show support for a #BlackOwnedBusiness.

#GREENNEWDEAL

Progressive Americans concerned about the environment have been pushing for a Green New Deal in one form or another since the early 2000s.

But more recently, during the decidedly un-environmentally friendly Trump presidency, Representative Alexandria Ocasio-Cortez and Senator Edward Markey, both Democrats, introduced a Green New Deal resolution that drew venom from Republicans and many other groups.

This Green New Deal calls for a shift away from fossil fuels to clean energy in an effort to both address climate change and create new jobs. If successful, it could kill two birds with one stone, at once saving the planet and solving some of society's great ills, such as economic inequality. It would not come cheap, however.

Needless to say, to date the effort has not met with success, but Ocasio-Cortez and Markey reintroduced the resolution in 2021. #GreenNewDeal continues to trend on social media, particularly whenever an extreme weather event wreaks havoc on the US, which is to say, with increasing frequency.

Green New Deals have met with more success in Europe, where Green parties have a longer history.

#MARCHFORSCIENCE

The election of Donald Trump to the US presidency set off unprecedented protesting from many groups in America, including scientists.

Some might say Trump did it to himself, charging that climate change is a hoax when he was still on the campaign trail and rolling back many environmental protection policies almost immediately after assuming the office. And he was hardly alone; many in his party supported him.

In April 2017, more than one million members of the scientific community, including scientists, teachers of science, and science believers, got together to #MarchForScience, demonstrating on the National Mall in Washington as well as in other cities around the world. Organizers were inspired by the monumental Women's March that had taken place earlier that year.

March for Science grew into a sophisticated movement that is nonpartisan but not apolitical. Along with its partners, it advocates for evidence-based policies around the world and for increased funding for scientific research.

#DREAMERS

Dreamers are the more than two million young, undocumented immigrants in America who would benefit from the DREAM Act, legislation that has kicked around Congress for many years but has not succeeded in becoming law. The DREAM Act stands for Development, Relief, and Education for Alien Minors, and it would provide a path to citizenship for these people.

Under the points of the latest iteration of the DREAM Act, called the American Dream and Promise Act, high school graduates and GED recipients could attain US citizenship through college, the armed forces, or work. Until such a bill is passed, millions of promising young people in America are in limbo, dreaming of a bright future in the only country most of them have ever known. They want to go on with their lives, pursuing careers and having families, but the threat of deportation is always just around the corner. They can only hope that Congress will make their dream a reality.